MOSAIC

WHEN GOD USES ALL THE PIECES

A Lenten Study for Adults

SHANE STANFORD

Abingdon Press
Nashville

MOSAIC
WHEN GOD USES ALL THE PIECES

Copyright © 2011 by Abingdon Press

This book is printed on acid-free paper.

All Scripture quotations, unless otherwise noted, are taken from the New Revised Standard Version of the Bible, copyright 1989, Division of Christian Education of the National Council of the Churches of Christ in the United States of America. Used by permission. All rights reserved.

Scripture quotations marked (NIV) are taken from the Holy Bible, New International Version®, NIV®. Copyright © 1973, 1978, 1984, 2011 by Biblica, Inc.™ Used by permission of Zondervan. All rights reserved worldwide. *www.zondervan.com.* The "NIV" and "New International Version" are trademarks registered in the United States Patent and Trademark Office by Biblica, Inc.™

Scripture quotations marked (*THE MESSAGE*) are taken from *THE MESSAGE*. Copyright © by Eugene H. Peterson 1993, 1994, 1995, 1996, 2000, 2001, 2002. Used by permission of NavPress Publishing Group.

Scripture quotations marked (NLT) are taken from the *Holy Bible*, New Living Translation, copyright © 1996, 2004, 2007. Used by permission of Tyndale House Publishers, Inc., Carol Stream, Illinois 60188. All rights reserved.

Library of Congress Cataloging-in-Publication Data

Stanford, Shane, 1970-
 Mosaic— : when God uses all the pieces : a Lenten study for adults / Shane Stanford.
  p. cm.
 ISBN 978-1-4267-1628-7 (pbk. : alk. paper) 1. Lent—Meditations. I. Title.
 BV85.S673 2011
 248.4—dc23

                                        2011037242

ISBN: 978-1-426-71628-7

11 12 13 14 15 16 17 18 19 20—10 9 8 7 6 5 4 3 2 1

MANUFACTURED IN THE UNITED STATES OF AMERICA

MOSAIC

For My Girls—

Masterpieces, Each One

CONTENTS

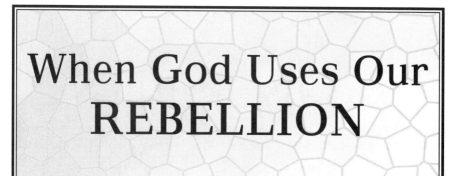

When God Uses Our REBELLION

"THE JAGGED EDGES"

In the days before D-Day, General Dwight D. Eisenhower's diary detailed the tense, difficult hours before the invasion. In some of the most personal and vulnerable descriptions of World War II, this great military leader described the fragile sense of waiting and how helpless he felt. His spirit was rattled with self-doubt and questions about whether the decision to invade on the Normandy coast in June of 1944 was the right decision. Eisenhower's statement to the soldiers was, "I have full confidence in your courage, devotion to duty and skill in battle. We will accept nothing less than full victory!"

Of course, we know how the story ends. The Allied invasion was successful, although many gave their lives in the process. It provided the foundation for what would be the death knell for Hitler's rule over Germany. The days that followed the invasion certainly accomplished their goal. But in many ways, the days before this huge undertaking defined not only its success, but also, if things had turned out differently, what could have been its incredible failure.

All of us have days before, jagged edges of our lives that mark the long journey for what it becomes, but also for how the pieces, broken apart by circumstance and mistake, either continue to cut our lives in two or become the eternal masterpiece of the Creator.

Over the course of this Lenten journey, we will look at how the God of the universe uses broken pieces, places, and people of our lives to create

God's artwork, a glistening masterpiece that reframes our potential and our purpose. This journey will take us along the same path Jesus walked in the days before and days along his own journey to Jerusalem. We will see the similarities to our own stories and the lessons we should pick up, like pebbles along the path.

In the end, we will not be the same. We shouldn't be. Any journey worth its value moves us to new places to accomplish new possibilities. That is God's point for you and for me—to recast the shards of discarded hopes and dreams into something beautiful and useful—a mosaic where God uses all of the pieces.

No Ordinary Day

Ash Wednesday is the name given to the first day of the season of Lent. In modern culture, it is known more for its implementation than for its history and meaning.

Ash Wednesday, originally called *dies cinerum* (day of ashes), is first mentioned in the eighth century. Early writings indicate that ashes were sprinkled on the head first, rather than anointed on the forehead as we practice today. But the meaning was the same—a reminder to us of our all-too-fragile lives.

The pouring of ashes on one's body served as an outer manifestation of an inner repentance or mourning. The earliest reference is found at the end of the Book of Job. Job, having been rebuked by God, confesses, "Therefore I despise myself, / and repent in dust and ashes" (Job 42:6). Other examples are found in Esther 4:1, 3; Isaiah 61:3; Jeremiah 6:26; and Daniel 9:3. In the New Testament, Jesus alludes to this practice in Matthew 11:21—"Woe to you, Chorazin! Woe to you, Bethsaida! For if the deeds of power done in you had been done in Tyre and Sidon, they would have repented long ago in sackcloth and ashes."

In the typical Ash Wednesday worship service, Christians come to the altar to receive the imposition of ashes. The pastor applies ashes in the shape of the cross on the forehead of each person who comes to the altar, while speaking the words, "You are dust, / and to dust you shall return" (Genesis 3:19). This is of course what God spoke to Adam and Eve after they fell into sin. In the context of the Ash Wednesday imposition of ashes, these words remind a person of their sinfulness and mortality, and thus their need to repent. The cross of ashes upon the forehead reminds each of us that through Jesus Christ, there is forgiveness for all sins.

Many Christians leave the ashes on their forehead for the remainder of the day. Of course, Jesus warned against religious practices that were meant to be showy (see Matthew 6:16-18). Rather, we wear the ashes as a witness that all people are sinners in need of Jesus for forgiveness through faith.

Ash Wednesday, like the season of Lent, is never mentioned in Scripture nor is it commanded by God. Christians are free to observe Ash Wednesday or not. It also should be obvious that the imposition of ashes is meaningless unless there is also an inner repentance.

The rite of ashes on Ash Wednesday is recommended to the Christian as an opportunity for repentance and spiritual renewal. It is the beginning of a journey that leads to the cross and an empty tomb; but it also prepares us for the journey ahead where we get not only a deeper glimpse of God, but also of each other and ourselves.

What follows in this section are four days of study, reflection, and prayer in the days before we begin our journey. These short devotions are meant to open your hearts and your minds to what God has in store during these next six weeks of Lent as we prepare for what the end of our journey through Jesus will reveal.

Your devotional time will reveal the heart of the lesson for the day, followed by a time for growing deeper through more questions and prayer. Take your time. These short focal points in your day are meant both to mark your map for the journey ahead and also to leave the crumbs from the baggage we set down and leave behind, in order that we never forget how far we have come.

REFLECT

Jesus taught mostly by questions: "Who do people say that I am?" "Where have they placed him [Lazarus]?" "Why should I give the food for the children to the dogs?" "Why are you so afraid [of the stormy seas]?" "Have you caught any fish?" "Do you have anything to eat?" Jesus used questions for two reasons. First, questions are nonthreatening. When talking about a person's tender places or confronting their rebellion, questions push into places "answers" cannot go. And second, questions open up a different sort of dialog among us. They help to move us beyond responding with a simple yes or no. Questions, at one stage or another, should move us into a deeper conversation meant to pierce our tough exterior, to a spirit perhaps laden with mistakes and regret, but also filled with amazing, divine possibilities.

And yet, there is one other critical benefit of questions as a teaching tool: identity. Questions allow us to confront our strengths and our weaknesses, reaching through both for a better way. Clearly Jesus uses our moments of greatest clarity and acceptance. But he also uses our moments of abject rebellion as well. It is this intersection where God finds the real you and the real me.

Don't worry, God has seen it all before, and nothing surprises him. In fact, God works best when our defenses are down. God knows the real you. Much like God's question to Adam and Eve after their fall, what God most wants is for *you to know where you are*.

I experienced this recently when my youngest daughter made a decision to jump from a particularly tall piece of play equipment at a local park. I had warned her not to jump, swing, or play past a certain height. "I can't reach you up there. If you fall, I won't be able to catch you," I said. But she chose to climb to that exact spot. And sure enough, she fell. She ended up with bruises on both arms and a pretty good bump on her head.

After making sure that she was OK, I questioned her: "What did I say to do? Why do you think I didn't want you to climb that high? Do you see now why I wanted you to be so careful?" You know, those sorts of questions.

After a few moments of conversation, we finally agreed that her decision to ignore my warnings had painful consequences that could (and should) have been avoided. She concluded that she didn't think she would try that again.

This reminded me of one of the most poignant scenes in the movie trilogy *The Lord of the Rings,* where the king of Rohan stands in the great hall of the kingdom before the major battle and asks, "How did it come to this?" Indeed.

God wants all of who we are—our rejoicing and our rebellion. These first days of our Lenten journey will prepare you to hand him both. You will be amazed at the questions God asks of you. You will be even more impressed with those you will begin to ask of yourself.

If Lent is indeed to remind us of our mortality, that from dust we came and to dust we shall return, just imagine what God might do when the "dust settles," when we find our place and hand him all of the pieces of the days before.

DAILY DEVOTIONS

Ash Wednesday

Scripture: Matthew 6:21

Wherever your treasure is, there the desires of your heart will also be.
(Matthew 6:21, NLT)

We are not enough. That may seem simple…overly so, in fact. But what does understanding our limits tell us about our potential?

The Bible is clear. We discover the most valuable places and parts of our lives when we stop and evaluate our "treasures"—not the monetary, earthly ones, but those aspects of our lives that truly, deeply matter to us (or at least should). For some, it might be our marriage; for others, our children; and still for others, our ambitions and possessions.

Yet even when we identify these places in our lives, something is missing. Jesus was clear that we are not enough, and that he fills a place in us that the world, although it might try, can never fill.

The odd, awkward truth about our "rebellion" from God is that what causes it is also what heals it. The need, the void where only God fits, that we yearn and struggle to fill with a variety of pleasures, people, places, and pursuits, ultimately has only one true answer—Jesus, our Savior, our Friend, our Example . . . our Treasure.

As we begin the journey of Lent, the real question emerges: Are the desires of your heart born from treasures worth the effort? Or do you seek more, crave more? Are you tired of running, working, reaching, begging for more, and yet never quite getting there?

God wants more for you. God has provided more for you. God, through Jesus, gave more for you. And that is enough.

Prayer
Gracious God, thank you for your grace and for your forgiveness when we run everywhere and in every direction but to you. Heal our hearts, redirect our paths, and engage our souls to want better, desire more, and seek for the treasure that is your love. We pray in Jesus' name. Amen.

Life Questions
Describe your "treasures." Why are they valuable? Are they worth the effort? Do your desires for them draw you closer to God or push you away from God?

Thursday

Scripture: Judges 2:10-15

Every time Israel went out to battle, the Lord fought against them, causing them to be defeated, just as he had warned. And the people were in great distress.

(Judges 2:15, NLT)

You've heard it said that "we are what we eat." Of course, we could also add, "And what we think . . . and what we fear . . . and what we desire." It goes on and on. Life is the byproduct of our crossroads, both good and bad.

The children of Israel experienced many crossroads. In this passage, the effects of disobedience unfold just one generation removed from Joshua's leadership. Of course, it only takes one generation, or less, when we discard the principles on which the foundation of our lives are built.

Moses and Joshua fought to keep the Israelites from becoming their own worst enemies. They weren't always successful. Their story unveils what we all face—namely the fragile places in each of our lives that get the best of us.

When we "forget our first love" (Revelation), we also miss the intimate ways that rejuvenate our souls. Live long enough in that pattern, and we set ourselves against God's disappointment and expectations, leading us farther and farther from God's will. The road becomes a dead end, and we find ourselves "in great distress."

That was not God's intention for his children. It is not God's intention for you. We are to grow every day more into God's likeness, not the likeness of the world. But when we miss the mark, we feel it, we know it . . . it is not normal.

God pushes back against our sin, against the broken places that lead us away from him. Do you feel resistance today? Do things seem to be working against you? Maybe that is less about circumstance and more about who God believes us to be—or at least, whom God believes in us to become.

Prayer

Gracious God, we are tired of running, tired of making the next step about ourselves instead of looking to you. We want more from life. We know that you have more in store for us. We pray that you will rescue us from the distress of our rebellion, in whatever forms it lives in us. Give us your heart, your direction at this crossroads of our lives. You believe in us. Help us to believe in ourselves. We pray in Jesus' name. Amen.

Life Questions

In what ways are you in "distress" today? How do these broken places keep you from seeking God's will for your life? How do they keep you from choosing God's new direction?

Friday

Scripture: Ezekiel 20:13-20

I am the LORD your God; follow my decrees and be careful to keep my laws. Keep my Sabbaths holy, that they may be a sign between us. Then you will know that I am the LORD your God."
(Ezekiel 20:19-20, NIV)

Ernest Gordon's *Miracle on the River Kwai* is the story of Scottish soldiers mistreated and abused by their Japanese captors during World War II. In fact, these particular Japanese soldiers were renegades and acted outside the established bounds of their own authority.

One day during a tool check, the count was off by one shovel. The guard demanded that the missing shovel be produced or he would kill the entire captive squad. People knew he meant it.

As he drew his gun to kill the first prisoner, a man stepped forward, basically admitting to having taken the shovel. The guard picked up an ax handle and beat the man to death. When the vicious scene ended, the other prisoners picked up the bloody corpse of their friend and moved to the next station, where another tool check was performed.

However, this time the count was perfect. The previous "missing shovel" had been a mistake. And yet, the man who had stepped forward had been willing to give his life for a "mistake" instead of allowing one of his men to be killed. The question of "who deserved what" meant little when life became so broken so quickly.

In Ezekiel, God's frustration with Israel is clear. They deserve God's anger, God's rejection. Their rebellion is profound and shocking. And yet, God gives them one more chance, even to the point of establishing a sabbath oath that would serve as a reminder (once per week) that God loved them more than he hated their sin.

That is our hope today. God's love, through Jesus, took on cosmic proportions when the cross and an empty grave became substitutes for what had broken our hearts for so long. God's Son stepped forward and took on our rebellion. It wasn't fair. It wasn't right. It wasn't logical. But it was amazing!

Prayer

Gracious God, we thank you for a love that doesn't make sense. We praise you for grace that doesn't seem possible. We love you for a new beginning that doesn't come fast enough. We know about our sin, about your grace, about our pain, about your love, and that you are our God; in Jesus' name. Amen.

Life Questions

In what ways do you "remember" God's promise for grace and forgiveness in your life? How do your actions and decisions point to God's place in your journey? In what ways do others see the "hands and feet of Jesus" in your world?

Saturday

Scripture: Jeremiah 3:19-22

I thought to myself, / "I would love to treat you as my own children!" / I wanted nothing more than to give you this beautiful land— / the finest possession in the world. / I looked forward to your calling me "Father," / and I wanted you never to turn from me.
(Jeremiah 3:19, NLT)

Not long ago, my middle daughter and I had climbed to the roof of the house to retrieve a remote controlled helicopter. Well, actually, she had climbed up there first before I saw what was happening and demanded that she stop right where she was. I hurried up the ladder, moving the greatest distance across the roof to grab the flying toy and then take measures to get us both off the roof. I told my daughter to stay at the edge, still on the ladder, holding tightly to the grips. I said that I would make my way to the ground first. I could then steady the ladder, and it would be safe for her to descend.

However, as my feet hit the ground, I heard my daughter say, "Hey, Dad, catch me!" No sooner had I looked up than my six-year-old daughter flew off the roof, heading directly for me.

I raised my arms just in time to catch her. However, the momentum knocked me off my feet, and we both tumbled to the ground.

After regaining my breath and composure, I looked intensely at my daughter and said, "Sweetheart, why did you do that?"

My daughter, with a slight gleam of the wonder and adventure still in her eyes, replied, "Because I knew you would catch me!" This was a simple, profound answer, albeit a painful one.

My daughter's faith in me was incredible. In fact, she had much more faith in me than I had in myself. She took the leap because she trusted that I would catch her.

Much of our rebellion, the Bible says, is the result of our fear and hesitancy, as much—if not more—than it is some need for adventure. Ultimately, we refuse to become all that God intends for us to be, because at the end of the conversation, we just can't believe God will catch us. Why would he? Haven't we disappointed him too many times?

Thank goodness God does not work that way. Not only does God catch us, but also he encourages us to "fly" into his arms and trust that his presence is sure and true.

Jeremiah reminds us that our relationship with God is personal to him. "I looked forward to your calling me 'Father' ... never to turn from me." How about you? Are you ready to leap from your brokenness and frustration? Are you ready to "fly" into God's new beginning?

Prayer

Gracious God, we are more hesitant to fly than you are to catch us. You continue to plead with us, "Do not be afraid...." Why can't we accept your promises? Give us courage to be still and to trust that you will catch us. We spend so much time, dear God, being so little, in spite of your giving us so much. We love you. Be patient with us; in Jesus' name. Amen.

Life Questions

What weights in life keep you grounded? How does God call you to "leap forward" today? In what ways are we afraid to "fly" into God's presence and become all that he has in store?

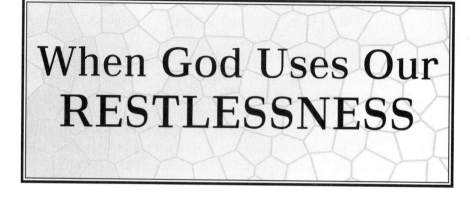

When God Uses Our RESTLESSNESS

Scripture: Read Matthew 11:28-30.

REVEAL

Several years ago, my wife and I moved to the Atlantic Coast to attend graduate school. We had lived in the humid, hot climate of South Mississippi our entire lives. Winters were modest by any standard, and I had experienced snow and ice only twice in my previous 21 years to that point.

So you can imagine my surprise when this area experienced a rare, powerful winter storm. They called it the "Storm of the Century." No one had remembered anything like it in at least two previous generations. The system left several inches of snow and ice on the roads and caused schools and government to come to a screeching halt.

We were told that this was rare but not unheard of for the area, which from time to time would experience powerful weather occurrences from systems rushing over the mountains and those coming from the Atlantic Ocean colliding. In any regard, rare or not, we had never seen anything like this back home in the Deep South.

From driving my car on the icy roads to watching the winter wonderland paralyze the infrastructure of the community, we were amazed at the power of weather.

For the next several days, we spent most of our time in the small apartment we rented in North Raleigh. It was a beautiful, wooded complex with "loft" configurations whereby the living area in the two-story apartment was on the top floor and the bedrooms on the bottom. It was larger than most other apartments but nowhere near the size of the large, old, lumbering parsonage from which we had moved just months before. And as the days stretched on, the size of the place seemed to shrink rapidly.

Of course, several factors played into our restlessness for those days. First, we had never experienced any weather pattern like this. Hurricanes, storms, flooding—all of that we had dealt with. But a winter storm had a different set of issues to confront. You felt trapped, not only in your space but because of the grinding halt to which the area found itself.

Second, the weather conditions changed so quickly. We were not prepared for temperatures in the low 60s and high 50s deteriorating over a matter of days into a major winter blast. To go from one extreme to the other caught us off guard.

Finally, we had things to do, things that we needed to take care of, or at least wanted to get started with or finish. Sure, at first the break was nice. We enjoyed spending the time together. It was a mini-vacation—for about 48 hours. But I was in theology school. My wife was a teacher. We were active leaders in our congregation. We had "to-do" lists, projects, and responsibilities. To have all of that suddenly stop, and remain so for an extended period of time, was unnerving to say the least.

The weather did not let up for several days. In fact, for nearly a week, this very unusual weather system pounded the East Coast, and in an extremely odd time of the year, left its mark for weeks to come. Thus, our restlessness grew. We became fractious, bored, frustrated, and impatient. And most of all, we began to direct these emotions and feelings toward each other. Thankfully, conditions finally improved and we were back to our routine. But we will never forget how our restlessness disrupted the rhythm of our lives.

When we become restless, the natural order of our lives is affected. We grow unsettled, and eventually our relationships suffer. Our responsibilities suffer as well. Psychologists say that a "restless mind" is nearly 40 percent less productive in terms of task accomplishment than a focused one. That seems self-evident, but when you think of how they define *restless,* the statistic becomes even more alarming. For this particular study, *restless* is defined as "any distraction created by emotional, relational, or physiological circumstances that prevents absolute focus on a task or responsibility." This is different from the impatience that comes when we are ready to do or accomplish more. No, actual restlessness is the exact opposite of living rested. It is the tired life—the frustrated life—the outdone life. As a pastor friend of mine likes to say, "It is the broken edge of our potential, and the stormy core of our discontent."

How many times a day do we catch ourselves thinking about the "other things" we have to take care of? Or how many times do our minds wander to conversations or relationships left undone? Restless is more than a state of mind or extended period; it is our disconnect between our potential and our reality.

Of course, restlessness happens at many levels; and most people are very productive as they manage their days, routines, and relationships, juggling the many balls that each of us has in the air at any given time. But what happens when the distractions gain more ground, when the other things take up more heart, time, or consideration? What happens when the balls begin to hit the ground?

The Bible is full of stories of individuals and groups of people who became distracted and lost their focus on God. Their restlessness gained ground in their lives, and the results were not good:

- ⊞ Jacob was restless and stole his brother's birthright.
- ⊞ Saul was restless and tried to kill his son's best friend . . . and the next king.
- ⊞ David was restless and took another man's wife for himself.
- ⊞ Jonah was restless and refused to preach forgiveness for Nineveh.
- ⊞ Nebuchadnezzar was restless and listened to corrupt advisors.
- ⊞ Peter was restless and nearly drowned.
- ⊞ Paul was restless and begged for the thorn to be removed.
- ⊞ And the stories continue.

Certainly, it is not unusual for us to grow restless. As you can see, some of the most faithful of God's servants fell prey to distractions that, in small and large ways, affected not only their lives but the lives and futures of those around them.

No, I don't believe most of us will allow our restlessness and distractions to cause us to murder. But what about adultery? What about greed? What about dishonesty? Yes, those hit closer to home and become more real. But none of those mentioned above woke up one morning and said, "Today, I believe I will mess up my life!" No, at some point along the way, their distraction became their destruction.

Remember the definition of *restless*—anything that keeps us from being wholly focused. . . . All of us have experienced that place in our daily walk where we feel less than wholly together. And unfortunately, we will, more than likely, face it again. But God has a better plan for our lives. God wants us to experience the focus of his grace and love, and to keep our lives on the path by which we become all that God has in store. Although God is more than aware of our fragile natures, God does not want one single moment whereby we miss what he desires to share with us.

In the examples above, God does not leave any of God's servants to their distractions. No, in fact, God uses their restlessness to address their condition, circumstances, and lack of focus, and provides a new path and destination. It wasn't always easy, nor was it always well-received by those in question. But in the end, the one receiving God's interaction saw the importance of trusting God's redirection in their lives. Let's chalk it up to being . . . restless.

The same is still true for us today. God uses our restlessness to bring us back to a better path. God reframes our potential and casts a new picture of what our focus should be. Don't allow the restlessness to push us along bumpy roads we were never intended to travel. God has a better journey planned.

REFLECT

People grow restless for three primary reasons. First, we confront an uncertain future, where we see the path but are unsure of what we will encounter. Second, we confront an unknown future, where we know the journey is ahead but can't see the path or its destination. Finally, we confront an unengaged future, where the road ahead becomes too long, passionless, and without purpose.

Think about it: How many marriages have faltered because of an unengaged future? How many work experiences have ended because of an unknown path? How many friendships come undone because too many turns in the road remain uncertain?

The restless life has long-lasting effects. For instance, the restless life loses its desire, energy, and passion. The more restless we grow, the wearier we get. It is like a spiritual adrenaline that, when used for the wrong purpose, dissolves quickly and is wasted. Our weariness flows from energy spent in areas that do not refill our hearts and souls.

Also, the restless life loses its way. We wander, many times far from those places and people who mean something to us, forgetting not only where we come from but also where we are going. And in response, we begin to trust every "point of reference" for our location except the one that matters most.

But God confronts our restlessness. In Matthew 11, Jesus tells his followers, "Come to me, all you who are weary and burdened, and I will give you rest" (verse 28, NIV). Most of us have heard this passage before. But it is the next part of the Scripture passage that may be the most important for God's remedy for our restlessness.

Jesus continues, "Take my yoke upon you and learn from me, for I am gentle and humble in heart, and you will find rest for your souls. For my yoke is easy and my burden is light" (verses 29-30, NIV). Did you hear what Jesus said?

First, Jesus said take a load off. You can't go forward with this burden. You need rest. Jesus provides rest for our souls and gives us the chance to regain our breath again.

But then Jesus encourages us to take his yoke upon us. The purpose of a yoke in Jesus' day was to guide an ox in its path. Many mistake a yoke for restraining the ox, but actually the opposite is true. It was a gift for the ox because as long as the ox remained in the yoke, he only had to trust its path. Jesus said my yoke is light . . . trust me and follow.

God provides a new desire for our hearts. God reignites our souls for his work and gives us his presence. But God also redirects our path and reestablishes our feet on firm ground—ground, unlike much of what the world offers, that leads somewhere. Our fear of the unknown, the uncertain, and the unengaged fades away with Christ's yoke of forgiveness, grace, and hope upon us.

Are you living a "heavy" life full of burdens? Do you feel lost? Are you restless, wondering what comes next or, even more importantly, why it even matters? God has something better in store for you. He wants to take the broken piece of restlessness and reframe it for a new creation, a mosaic of a new masterpiece.

REFINE

Read Psalm 46:10; Jeremiah 50:34; Matthew 11:28-30;
Luke 21:34; and John 4:11-13; 6:35.

1. **Examine:** After reading the suggested Scriptures, examine what God is saying through these passages concerning your situation. What does God say about the problem of restlessness? How do the passages of Scripture provide a new path and potential for how we confront the restlessness of our lives?

2. **Identify:** Identify the problem of restlessness in your life. How has it affected your relationships? How does restlessness affect the way you see God and serve him? How does restlessness affect the way you view the future and opportunities? Provide as detailed an explanation for the issue that holds you back.

3. **Define:** Define what a solution would look like if God dealt with your restlessness. Many times, our inability to take hold of God's gift of healing, new direction, or second chance is our struggle in naming what those characteristics look like in our lives. We become so focused on the problem that we forget what a solution might entail. What will your relationships look like? What new opportunities will come your way? How will you serve God better? Define your solution. Be as specific as possible. Paint an unmistakable picture of how God reframes your broken piece called restlessness into a beautiful new masterpiece.

4. **Name:** Name the steps to achieve that solution. What would that desired future for God's new reality in your life require of you? What changes do you need to make to begin the process? What old patterns need addressing? What new habits should you take up? Name the process that becomes God's path to reshape your potential and your life.

5. **Commit:** Commit to an action plan to make God's plan your reality. When do you start? Who goes with you? How do you begin? Now start!

RESPOND

The following daily reading schedule provides insight for addressing the restlessness in your life. The goal is to watch God take the weary burdens that keep you from your path in God and reshape your potential and possibilities.

Study Suggestions
1. Read each day's Scripture passage.
2. List the principle lessons of that day's Scripture.
3. Describe how the principles can be applied to your daily life.
4. Journal your thoughts, feelings, and impressions. Include a list of prayer requests, praises, and concerns.

Monday: Numbers 20:1-13
Tuesday: Ecclesiastes 12:13-14
Wednesday: Romans 5:1-2
Thursday: Ephesians 2:14-18
Friday: Mark 8:11-13
Saturday: Philippians 4:6-7

Prayer
Gracious God, we pray for the places in our lives where we are restless, where the pulse of our fear, doubt, and brokenness keeps us from finding rest. We give these places to you and trust that having turned them over our souls might find wholeness again. We close our eyes, take a deep breath, and set down the baggage. You are our rest. We love that you see us so differently than we oftentimes see ourselves. Thank you for taking this broken, jagged piece of our souls and for creating a beautiful masterpiece; in Christ. Amen.

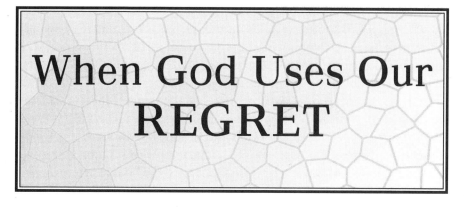

When God Uses Our REGRET

Scripture: Read Psalm 51:1-15 and Luke 19:1-8.

REVEAL

Not long ago, my family went with friends on their beautiful houseboat for an afternoon voyage across the bay in the ocean town where we lived. We would anchor at a private stretch of sand not far from the pass of the bay that led to the Gulf of Mexico. Passes are notoriously rough, with high waves and deadly currents negotiating the flow of water through the narrow opening. We decided to stay on the bayside of the beach where the waters were safe and calm. We anchored several hundred feet from the shore, watching the drift and depth of the boat before setting the anchor line not far from the beach. At that point, in the lazy, sunny afternoon, we set out simply to have a good time with friends, food, and fellowship.

For several hours, we watched the weather, seeing few clouds, and made sure that the boat remained in place. It was a comfortable day with great friends. There was a steady breeze but nothing out of the ordinary.

Some time after dinner, as we sat in the spacious cabin talking about a variety of issues, our friend, the captain, jumped from his seat and moved quickly to the controls. As we stood to see what was happening, we were shocked to discover that the boat, in just a matter of twenty minutes or so, had been pushed dangerously close to the shore. The winds had increased significantly and had, in a matter of minutes, created a strong wave current for the shore.

In the large houseboat, we had not felt the sudden increase of the waves and the strong current that developed as the winds pushed everything on the open bay toward the beach. By the time my friend addressed the helm, the boat was in serious danger of running aground.

He engaged the motors. The thrusters rattled the boat as we struggled to release from the sandy bed below the surface. Our friend worked with the boat for nearly 30 minutes. At times, it appeared that we were making headway, only to have the winds push us back from whatever ground we gained.

Finally, as the winds died at just the right moment, the boat found enough momentum to push out from the shore and the powerful propellers roared. We were free from the sandy bottom, moving farther and farther into the bay.

Everyone on the boat let out a loud cheer—everyone but our friend, the captain. I could tell that he was still fighting with the controls. As I walked over to inquire, I watched as he moved the wheel back and forth with great effort.

"We've damaged the rudder," my friend said. "I am not sure I can control it going into dock." Of course, those words concerned me. In our joy of breaking free from the shoreline, I had not thought about the damage we might have taken on under the boat in the process.

"What do we do?" I asked.

"Not much beyond 'wait and see,'" my friend replied. "We will only know the damage below by how she reacts on the surface." How true.

Eventually, my friend navigated our struggling boat back to dock. Sure enough, the rudder had been significantly damaged, and he was able to control the boat only through using the motors to stir. My friend is an excellent captain, but even with his skills, the damage below created a lot of trouble for us above.

As we disembarked, unloading supplies and materials, my friend looked at me and said, "I sure regret not keeping my eye on the shore."

"It all happened so fast," I replied.

"Yes, but an experienced captain knows that the winds can rise at any moment and push us aground," my friend said. "The first thing a good seaman learns is to keep an eye on surroundings, for you will certainly regret it if you don't."

We learned a valuable lesson that day. We learned about the power of the open water, and why you never let your guard down. The most difficult regrets on the water are the ones that come from decisions and moments when we should know better.

Later, as our family gathered for our evening devotion, we talked about the incident on the boat. My youngest daughter was the first to answer when I asked what we had learned from it.

"You can't let your guard down," she said.

"No, you can't," I replied.

"The winds and waves came when we least expected it," she continued.

"They always do," was my reply. "They always do."

REFLECT

Regret is a difficult burden to bear. It is different from restlessness. Restlessness is the undoing of our focus, the impediment that keeps us from accomplishing the full measure of what God has in store. As we discussed in the last lesson, God uses our restlessness by getting our attention and by challenging us to learn from and follow him. Restlessness is more of a directional issue than a weight, more easily remedied as we take Christ's yoke upon us.

Regret is heavier, more encumbering. It is not easily shaken, and when allowed to grow and take hold, it will choke not only our potential but also our joy. Certainly, the world is filled with regret, and no life is immune from it. But as the apostle Paul states in Second Corinthians, what the world intends for our brokenness, God can transform into a holy moment. "Godly sorrow [regret] brings repentance that leads to salvation and leaves no regret" (2 Corinthians 7:10, NIV). But the contrary is also true. When left unchecked, sorrow and regret carried outside of God's grace and forgiveness burden us until we find little purpose. It becomes the lens by which we see our world, and the scales by which we measure our hope.

Regret affects us for several reasons. First, regret steals our joy. I have counseled many people over the years who can't see past their mistakes.

One young lady, in particular, met me in the bullpen (the place near the stage where we talked with guests after services) and was clearly struggling with something emotional. She told me of decisions and mistakes made that had dominated her life for many years. As we talked and prayed together, I will never forget her final words. "The worst of it all," she said, "is that I can't remember why it matters anyway." Regret steals our joy.

Second, regret steals our potential. Regret paralyzes the gifts and future that God has in store for us. Its purpose is to leave us stuck in the muck of our mistakes and to convince us that we have no other options. It reminds me of the story of cave explorers in the 1920s who died in a particularly difficult cave system in Costa Rica. When rescuers found their bodies, they could tell that the group had worked to free themselves from the caves; however, they gave up, believing that they had no hope. Unfortunately, the rescuers located their final resting place just 30 yards from a tight but workable cavern to freedom. Regret traps us and convinces us that there is no hope. Regret steals our potential.

Finally, regret steals our purpose. Regret convinces us that, because of one circumstance or another, God can't use us any longer. Many people believe the driving force, the engine, of a person are the things we can collect or consume. But I like what Charles Kingsley, in *Bits & Pieces,* says: "We act as though comfort and luxury were the chief requirements of life, when all that we need to make us really happy is something to be enthusiastic about" (Charles Kingsley, *Bits & Pieces,* December 9, 1993, p. 16.). However, take away that passion, the purpose of why a person gets up in the morning—or even simply damage it with regret—and we seriously hinder a person's ability to do much else.

To echo Paul in Romans 8, "What shall we say about such things?"

God has a plan for taking the broken pieces of our regrets and placing them into a beautiful new masterpiece. And although we struggle to see them as more than jagged edges of what should have been, God sees our potential from another angle, and God doesn't regret investing in our future.

Zacchaeus

No story in Scripture exemplifies God's plan for restoring our regrets into potential better than Zacchaeus.

Zacchaeus was not welcomed as he weaved in and out of the crowds, trying to catch a glimpse of Jesus. The crowd despised Zacchaeus. He was a tax collector for Rome; his transgression was considered a betrayal of the core of Jewish culture. And as a tax collector goes, Zacchaeus was not just any run-of-the-mill official—he was a prized part of the Roman establishment. However, to the Jewish citizens of Jericho, Zacchaeus was a traitor. He had achieved great power and wealth, but at what price? He was one of the most hated men in the city, epitomizing the image of someone who possessed everything but had nothing. It was a life of great and painful contrasts: the best of the world's bounty, the worst of the soul's distress. We know little about Zacchaeus's past. What we do know is that Zacchaeus, for one reason or another, had chosen this life and, as is often the case with those like him, found himself in a pattern that, over time, offered little in the way of better alternatives.

Still, Zacchaeus sought something different. Maybe he heard about Jesus and his teachings, about how he loved the sinners and ate with outcasts. Maybe there was enough of a desire for the "other road," the one less traveled, in Zacchaeus that he believed getting a glimpse of Jesus might create a miracle. We'll never know. Regardless, we find him weaving through the hateful crowd, vying for an opportunity to see the Teacher from Nazareth. Zacchaeus was many miles down a lonesome, twisted road of regrets and mistakes, and may have believed that Jesus would never associate with him. But what if he would? Zacchaeus determined that the risk was worth it, that maybe, unlike what everyone else in that crowd believed, he was not too far gone for something to change—that his potential was not completely gone.

No, the voice deep within us, no matter how far we have wandered, echoes our longings for new directions and possibilities. I'm sure that Zacchaeus could never have imagined how his day would turn out. Who could? Getting a glimpse of Jesus is one thing; having him invite himself to dinner at your house—no way! (But we're getting ahead of ourselves.)

Whatever he was thinking that day, however he imagined the outcome, Zacchaeus did the only thing we are asked to do: He made his way to the street and waited to see if there was any truth to what he had heard about this Jesus—if someone like Jesus could look past his regret and love even him.

When Jesus saw Zacchaeus sitting in the tree, he stopped and called him by name: "Zacchaeus, come down. Today, I will eat at your house" (see Luke 19:5). Can you imagine the shock, not only for Zacchaeus, but

29

also for the entire crowd? Did Jesus just speak to Zacchaeus? Did he just say that he was eating dinner at Zacchaeus's house? But Jesus knew exactly what he was doing. Let's face it, Jesus is a "name-caller"; and the name he likes most is our own. Throughout the Gospels, we hear of Jesus calling people by name—and not just the religious folks, either. No, Jesus spent time calling the names of people who hadn't heard their names spoken in a welcoming tone in quite a while. He knew the power of giving people dignity in order to later change their potential. It had probably been a long time since someone had called Zacchaeus by name without connecting it to some form of profanity or curse. To hear his name spoken by Jesus, of all people, must have been like hearing beautiful music. However, Jesus was not only a name-caller; he also liked a good party. We know because he was always inviting himself to one. And why not? What better place to get to know someone than around a table, sharing a good meal with good friends? Jesus liked to enter into people's space and get to the heart of who they were. He couldn't have cared less about what the religious folks and the social elite thought. Jesus wanted to know the real insides of people so that he could fill those empty places with something of real value—no more mistakes, no more regrets. Jesus defines us by something more, something better. By calling Zacchaeus's name, Jesus gave Zacchaeus an identity; by going to his home, Jesus gave Zacchaeus a future.

Zacchaeus's response surprised those around him, but it shouldn't surprise us. We read the rest of the story and know what happens when sinners encounter the love of Jesus: The change can't be contained. It is overwhelming, and it causes people to do crazy things, like give away their possessions and try to make things right. Zacchaeus did the only thing he could have done. Zacchaeus exploded in gratitude and thanksgiving. He gave back to those who he had wronged, not once or twice but four times what he owed them. Freedom from what binds us makes people do amazing things. Even more wonderful, though, was Jesus' proclamation. After Zacchaeus responded, Jesus declared, "Today, salvation has come to this house, because this man, too, is a son of Abraham" (see Luke 19:9). Jesus restored him to the family. Zacchaeus was no longer an outcast or orphan; he belonged. It means everything. God's goal in drawing close to us through Jesus is not just that we might confront our regrets and know our sin, but also that God might transform our lives and make us new.

Jesus did several things in confronting Zacchaeus that day on the road to Zacchaeus's house, and he wants to do those same things for you and for me. Wouldn't it be nice to have someone call your name without feeling as though you were a suspect? Or what about experiencing real fellowship, the kind where you know you really belong? Maybe, then, it would change your heart or my heart, so much so that we would do the unthinkable, doing more than just proclaiming the joy again but actually working to make it so. Talk about a game changer—new potential with *real* purpose.

That is what happens when Jesus confronts our regrets. This is no accident; it is no mistake. And you will never regret that he did.

REFINE

Read 1 Samuel 15; Psalm 33; Isaiah 43; Mark 11:24;
Luke 19:1-10; Philippians 3:13-15; and 1 Peter 5.

1. **Examine:** After reading the suggested Scriptures, examine what God is saying through these passages concerning your situation. What does God say about the problem of living with regrets? How do the passages of Scripture provide a new path and potential for how we confront the areas of regret for our lives?

2. **Identify:** Identify the power of regret in your life. How has it affected your relationships? How do your current regrets affect the way you see God and serve him? How do regrets affect the way you view the future and opportunities? Provide as detailed an explanation for the issue that holds you back.

3. **Define:** Define what a solution would look like if God truly dealt with your regrets. Many times, our inability to take hold of God's gift of healing, new direction, or second chance is our struggle in naming what those characteristics look like in our lives. We become so focused on the problem that we forget what a solution might entail. What will your relationships look like? What new opportunities will come your way? How will you serve God better? Define your solution. Be as specific as possible. Paint an unmistakable picture of how God reframes your broken piece called regret into a beautiful new masterpiece.

4. **Name:** Name the steps to achieve that solution. What would that desired future for God's new reality in your life require of you? What changes do you need to make to begin the process? What old patterns need addressing? What new habits should you take up? Name the process that becomes God's path to reshape your potential and your life.

5. **Commit:** Commit to an action plan to make God's plan your reality. When do you start? Who goes with you? How do you begin? Now start!

RESPOND

The following daily reading schedule provides insight for addressing the regret in your life. The goal is to watch God take the weary burdens that keep you from your path in God and reshape your potential and possibilities.

Study Suggestions
1. Read each day's Scripture passage.
2. List the principle lessons of that day's Scripture.
3. Describe how the principles can be applied to your daily life.
4. Journal your thoughts, feelings, and impressions. Include a list of prayer requests, praises, and concerns.

Monday: Psalm 51:1-15
Tuesday: Matthew 27:3-10
Wednesday: 2 Samuel 12:1-23
Thursday: 2 Corinthians 7:10
Friday: Ezekiel 6:8-11
Saturday: John 9:35-41

Prayer
Gracious God, we pray for places where our regrets continue to taunt us and remind us that we are all too human. Our fragile lives look so broken against the backdrop of our mistakes and the standards of this world. But you love us anyway. You take our regrets and reframe our place in

your family. You are our place of confidence, our place of no regret. We love that you see us so differently than we oftentimes see ourselves. Thank you for taking this broken, jagged piece of our souls and for creating a beautiful masterpiece; in Christ. Amen.

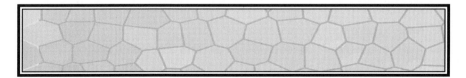

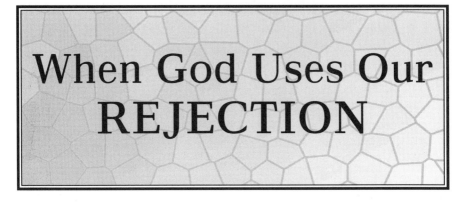

When God Uses Our REJECTION

Scripture: Read Matthew 9:12-13; 27:27-31;
and 1 Peter 5:7.

REVEAL

A pastor friend recently left his appointment as senior pastor of a moderate- sized church. It was not an "easy leave," as they call it. The spirit of the congregation was apathetic at best, and antagonistic in reality. The lay leadership spent the last few weeks of my friend's tenure making life difficult for him. They suspended his professional account, required his family to move out of the parsonage two weeks early in order to begin renovations, and then submitted my friend a bill for certain cleanings and improvements. By the time he and his family had the church and the town in their rearview mirror, they were exhausted and hurt—exhausted from the constant sparring with hurting people bent on hurting him, and hurt that those who were supposed to care for him allowed such broken places to erupt.

I have heard it said that "nothing is more perfect on this planet than when the local church is working right." But the opposite of that is also true. Nothing is more broken, more imperfect than when the local church does not work right. And this is not an institutional matter or issue. No,

I am talking about the "Church"—our brothers and sisters in the faith, who, for good or bad, are our family . . . our people. The "Church" is the framework for how God's grace becomes our reality. Therefore, when those relationships break down, it affects all of us. That is why my pastor friend's situation felt so bad even to those of us who were not directly involved. We believe things are supposed to be different among God's children, although Scripture does not testify to such.

Maybe that is what has burdened my friend more than anything else. The details of his treatment are not nearly as painful as the characters and setting involved.

As we have talked with my friend over the last months, walking with him through these latest, difficult circumstances with this congregation, the one question everyone asks is "Aren't you angry with the rejection your congregation has shown you?" To the world, and to most of his friends, the answer seems obvious. And from time to time, our friend has expressed the same sentiment, questioning both his own decision but also God's in bringing him to the church in the first place.

But my friend has mostly viewed the last couple of years from a much different perspective than most of us would have thought or considered. When we ask those questions of him, he will respond by saying, "Sure, there is always a part of me that will question that, until . . ." The *until* is followed by a litany of amazing things that happened in people's lives and families after he arrived at that church.

There is the story of the family who lost their young child to a car accident just weeks after our friend arrived as pastor. My friend spent countless hours with them, holding their hands and praying for them as they grieved, struggled, and remembered.

Or the story of the widow who lives in the apartments just across the street from the church who showed up at my friend's office his first day on the job to give him a homemade pound cake. She had been widowed for nearly 60 years, when the love of her life died at the Battle of the Bulge. The pound cakes continued, as did the conversations and the wonderful stories from an amazing woman's even more amazing journey.

Maybe it is the story of the couple whose marriage came apart just before the husband would meet my friend at the local Starbucks. My friend noticed that something was wrong, and a three-hour conversation ensued. The couple, with the help of my friend, agreed to marriage counseling, and now are on the road to healing.

Yet maybe it is the story of the young woman in her late twenties who took her first Communion at a service my friend administered. She received the bread from my friend and then plunked (that is the best word for it) the bread into the cup. The young woman lifted the element out of the cup and held it in front of her face before she ate it. The look on her face was incredible, as she truly studied what she was about to do. The young woman had many challenges in her life, but on that day, she became an example of why we should all pause and be in awe of Christ's body and blood.

My friend would tell these stories and others, testaments to the working of the Holy Spirit behind the scene and under the surface of what appeared a tragic drama and stormy sea. We could tell dozens more. And each of them occurred at the church during the time that my friend was their pastor. With all the difficulties, the discourteous behavior, the un-Christian responses, God continued to do amazing things.

So at the end of every time my friend received that question about the rejection of his congregation, he would answer, "No. Because no matter what, God showed up."

REFLECT

In Matthew 27, the story of Jesus' betrayal, arrest, and crucifixion is one filled with rejection. From Judas's attempt to give back the thirty pieces of silver to the Pharisees to the death of Jesus, one story after another fills quickly with far too much of humanity's faults.

One especially powerful section in the chapter begins in verse 27, when the soldiers at the foot of the cross mock and abuse Jesus. Their taunts and treatment of Jesus are difficult to read. Anyone who has been the butt of a joke or has endured the sneers of people knows how personal those encounters are. Take the setting of the Crucifixion, and it is multiplied by infinity.

As a literary bystander to the scene, one cannot help but wonder what kind of people would do that. How could they stand there and treat another person, even one in that situation, with such disdain and cruelty? I can only imagine what the scene must have been like for the women who stood just a few feet away watching their friend, son, and brother die, all while these men levied such attacks on him. Certainly, they came to their senses. After all, doesn't one of them confess the lordship of Jesus by the end?

In Christian tradition, it is interesting to discover that the story of the guards in particular occupies a lot of conversation for early Christian scholars and theorists. Stories from various histories and apocryphal accounts of the Crucifixion can't seem to leave these men to their hatred and cruel spirits. One account has them confessing Jesus as Lord. Another connects them to the centurion who is converted by Philip, while another story actually gives the guard who speared Jesus a name, Longinus, and makes his story of repentance and restoration very personal. Of course, most Christian historians will tell you that we do not know for certain what happened to these soldiers. But we want to think it turned out different. Even for the fate of someone so cruel, it is difficult to live with the prospect of the ultimate rejection for eternity.

Maybe more than any other lesson, the lesson of regret turns the pages on our story's rougher themes. To have been so close to the Divine and to have missed it—well, isn't that the story of everyone in our lives who has turned the wrong way or proceeded down the wrong the path? Left to ourselves, we either edit the story to fit our conscience or reshape the destination so that the regret doesn't feel so bad.

But as my pastor friend has said many times, "People disappoint each other, and church folks are better at it than anyone." He is so right. The real story of God's love is not that God spends so much time working to address our rejection, but that we spend so much time trying to pretend it doesn't matter.

Certainly, it matters that my friend's church has treated him so poorly. Certainly, it matters that people make horrible decisions that affect how others see themselves, the world, and God. Certainly, it matters that words we wish we had not said, and actions we wish we had not done, oftentimes reshape our path and future relationships. Certainly, it mattered that soldiers cruelly mocked an innocent man. Certainly, it mattered that while they mocked him, his friends ran and hid. Certainly, rejection matters.

We would all like to believe that our actions and words have no consequence, because that would mean that no one we love and no innocent bystander would ever become the victim of our selfishness or callous disregard for a better choice. But such is life. And without any further redemption of our stories, we live with the rejection that piles on top of us like boulders intent on pushing and keeping us down.

But God does not allow the story to end there. Throughout Scripture, God intervenes in the midst of humanity's rejection of itself, of God, of each other, and reframes the picture. We see a new beginning or a different path from what the world considers our only outcome. God believes all situations are redeemable, all lives matter, and all stories are just one page from a new chapter.

I suspect that most of our rejection happens when we try to measure our lives much like on a scale of one to ten, with one being the place where we feel forgotten and alone and ten being the place where we are perfectly connected, having gotten everything right. God doesn't share his love on the basis of a number. God doesn't love pastors any more than lay people. God doesn't love tall people more than he does short ones. God doesn't have a special place in his heart for the winner of beauty pageants and doesn't give points on the basis of how far a man can throw a baseball. And maybe more importantly, God doesn't love the "good" people any more than he loves the "bad" people.

Jesus said that healthy people didn't need a physician and that he came to call the sick and the sinners (Matthew 9:12-13). If the only way I can know the Great Physician is to be sick, then what makes me think I can make myself well alone?

If you look at the context of what Jesus is saying about the relationship between the well and the sick, think about how most people who are ill in our society are treated. If the sickness is acute and quick, most people respond with care. Many, if not most of us, have someone who will care for us during bouts of illness. But what happens if the illness becomes chronic? What happens if the cure is not easy or quick? What happens if the diagnosis for the world is more serious and, heaven forbid, terminal?

The unfortunate answers are that people change when the illness becomes more serious. People who had been there during the acute stage fall away when the illness drags on. Others do not know what to do with the consequences of illness. Those who are chronic or terminal oftentimes are placed where they can have little impact on the "healthy" person's normal routine. I have watched it over and over again. A loved one will become sick with some debilitating illness. Their entire routine changes. Their ability to care for themselves changes. They become more burden than blessing, and, before long, once caring, supportive family members are talking in hushed tones and rolling their eyes at how *all* of their lives have changed. It is a normal, if not uncomfortable, response to these situations.

The result is rejection. OK, maybe the family member doesn't walk away or abandon the person who is sick (although that happens far too many times). But the relationship changes. One friend of mine said that we are blessed in this world if we have one or two people who will love us through the sickest of our days. I understand. I am blessed.

But many folks are not, and they, the elderly, the person with AIDS lie in their hospital beds in convalescent homes across this nation, wondering what they did to face the rejection of their loved ones. The cost of rejection is even more personal when our "illness" is sin, when our disease is being far too human.

I am reminded of a sermon I heard once where the preacher said that our churches were too often places where people had to bandage their wounds and walk upright before they could be welcomed. We sit around as though no one has a problem; all the while our souls are bleeding to death under our nice, neat facades.

But if Jesus were to come to our community, he would not land in our churches. He would visit the hospitals, the convalescent homes, the city streets and back alleys looking for those whose wounds are too deep to bandage. Jesus would find those most rejected, because he was rejected as well.

It is only at the place of rejection that I can really know God's love. Love in response to goodness (or right decisions, or obedience, or wise actions) isn't love. That's reward. Love can only be demonstrated in the face of that which isn't lovely. When I look back, it is the valley of rejection where I discovered God's grace and love most.

It would be nice not to have any rejection. But then if I had no rejection, I would never grow. Rejection is a sign of two things. First, it is a sign of the imperfect world in which we live, and secondly, it is a sign that God wants to bridge the gap the keeps us from him.

What is your rejection that you can't let go? Just go to God and give him that place of rejection in your life. It makes whatever caused the rejection seem to be a gift of God's love—yes, I know that might be difficult. But God will love you no matter what and clean up the mess. God will love you through the emotion and brokenness. Rejection doesn't get the last word with God. Such is grace. Such is forgiveness. Such is a life brought back from the edge.

REFINE

Read Matthew 9:12-13; 27:27-31; Acts 13:50-52;
Romans 11:14-16; and 1 Peter 5:7.

1. **Examine:** After reading the suggested Scriptures, examine what God is saying through these passages concerning your situation. What does God say about the problem of living with rejection? How do the passages of Scripture provide a new path and potential for how we confront the areas of rejection for our lives?

2. **Identify:** Identify the power of rejection in your life. How has it affected your relationships? How do your current areas of rejection affect the way you see God and serve him? How does rejection affect the way you view the future and opportunities? Provide as detailed an explanation for the issue that holds you back.

3. **Define:** Define what a solution would look like if God truly dealt with your rejection. Many times, our inability to take hold of God's gift of healing, new direction, or second chance is our struggle in naming what those characteristics look like in our lives. We become so focused on the problem that we forget what a solution might entail. What will your relationships look like? What new opportunities will come your way? How will you serve God better? Define your solution. Be as specific as possible. Paint an unmistakable picture of how God reframes your broken piece called rejection into a beautiful new masterpiece.

4. **Name:** Name the steps to achieve that solution. What would that desired future for God's new reality in your life require of you? What changes do you need to make to begin the process? What old patterns need addressing? What new habits should you take up? Name the process that becomes God's path to reshape your potential and your life.

5. **Commit:** Commit to an action plan to make God's plan your reality. When do you start? Who goes with you? How do you begin? Now start!

RESPOND

The following daily reading schedule provides insight for addressing the rejection in your life. The goal is to watch God take the weary burdens that keep you from your path in God and reshape your potential and possibilities.

Study Suggestions
1. Read each day's Scripture passage.
2. List the principle lessons of that day's Scripture.
3. Describe how the principles can be applied to your daily life.
4. Journal your thoughts, feelings, and impressions. Include a list of prayer requests, praises, and concerns.

Monday: Isaiah 53:1-12
Tuesday: John 8:1-11
Wednesday: John 14:15-26
Thursday: Romans 8:38
Friday: John 6:37
Saturday: Hebrews 13:5

Prayer
Gracious God, we pray for places where we have been rejected or, by fault or forgetting, we have rejected others. You take away the sting of loneliness and of not belonging by making us part of you. You call us to your table; share the bounty of your grace, love, and forgiveness; and welcome us home. You are our open door and our safe harbor. We love that you see us so differently than we oftentimes see ourselves. Thank you for taking this broken, jagged piece of our souls and for creating a beautiful masterpiece; in Christ. Amen.

When God Uses Our
RESPONSIBILITIES

Scripture: Read Genesis 3:12-13 and John 14.

REVEAL

Late one Saturday afternoon, my wife and I received the call that all parents dread. Our middle daughter had been in a serious car accident. The voice of the officer was determined and straightforward. "Sir, your daughter has been involved in an accident," he said. "How serious is it?" I responded. "The car is totaled," he began. My stomach dropped. "But your daughter is fine," he finished. "She has some bumps and bruises, but should be OK."

They took our daughter to the local hospital. Although the hospital was some two hours away, we immediately got into our car and made our way to our daughter's side. When we arrived there, we were ushered back through the emergency room main doors to the cubicle where our daughter was resting. True to form, she had some bruises and cuts in various places, but overall she looked fine. We felt very blessed. We hugged our daughter, and kissed her on the forehead. Nothing else in the world mattered to us at that moment other than our little girl being safe.

Over the course of the next few hours, as the doctors observed our daughter to make sure that there were no other issues, another young girl arrived in the cubicle next to us. She, too, had been in an accident; but it wasn't a wreck with another vehicle. No, this young lady, I learned later, had attempted an overdose. She could not have been more than sixteen years old.

The cubicles' walls were paper-thin, and the sound from one to another traveled unhindered. A conversation in one cubicle was clearly understood in another; and whether you wanted to or not, you *would* know the situation of the person in the next cubicle.

As the doctors addressed the physical needs of the young lady, they also asked about her family or friends who might come and be at her side, the way we had rushed to our daughter's side. But she could not (or would not) give them an answer, and no one arrived over the course of the next hours.

The young lady was stubborn, to say the least. You could tell that her attempt to end her life was more a cry for help than an attack on her body. Her soul was damaged far worse than her body was, and, by the tones of her answers, you could tell that she was angry with people and places that, deep inside of her, she believed had led her here.

The more the doctors and social workers asked about her next of kin and her personal information, the more walls she built, until finally she was hidden away emotionally behind rage, pain, and disappointment. One of the nurses, who knew that I was a pastor (I had pastored in that area several years earlier), asked if I might help with "connecting" with the young lady. Having heard much of what the doctors and hospital officials had dealt with in the couple of hours before, I doubted I could make any more headway, but agreed to try.

The young lady was difficult ... and scared. I saw through her tough exterior. She was not unlike countless other young people I had seen over the course of my ministry who had done very grown-up things but were still, in truth, very un-grownup themselves. Behind her harsh tones and jagged words, she was a beautiful little girl, not much older than my oldest daughter. Given a few less nights where she cried herself to sleep wondering if her mother would come home, or a few less days mourning a father who, although not dead in body, was very much gone in spirit, her life would look very much like my own little girl.

But at the end of the day, this young lady stood at the crossroads of her life and wondered if it would not be better to just end it all. The young lady and I talked for a while until it was time for me to take my own daughter home. I shared how at sixteen I learned horrible news that told me I would not live to see my eighteenth birthday. She listened, but I could tell she also heard me. There's a difference. I believe that she appreciated the honesty of knowing that my life had not been easy either, and that I had faced situations that pushed me to the brink. I also told her that it would help her to listen to the good people trying to help her and that not all adults would let her down. I am not sure she really believed the last part but she, at least, nodded yes.

This was a little girl who fell through the cracks for the people whose responsibility it was to make sure she had what she needed, beginning with hugs, safety, and a place to call home. From what I could get her to tell me, she had very little of any of these, and mostly she bounced from apartment to apartment with a mom who spent more time looking for the next boyfriend than making sure her daughter was OK. Unfortunately, this young lady was taking on the same view of life that her mother probably had, although she would never admit it, reminding me that we often become what we value in this world. No one inherits the consequences of our broken promises and misguided responsibilities more than our children do.

To highlight this point, two little girls sat just a few feet from each other in a hospital emergency room. They were connected by more than just their need for medical treatment. Both little girls were the byproducts of how those who were supposed to take care of them had lived up to that responsibility. They were both the beneficiaries of the promises and gifts that we had come through on or had broken. And both little girls were the heirs to lifetimes of other people's successes or failures.

I packed up my daughter's things and walked behind her to the door of the emergency room. I took one glance back at the little girl in the adjoining cubicle and noticed that another social worker was standing by her bed. The scowl I had seen when I walked in was back, and the defenses were employed once again. I reached down and put my hand on my little girl's head. She reached up with her own hand and touched mine. As the nurse helped us out the door, I told her to wait here and I would bring the car around. My daughter smiled and said, "Sure, Daddy. I will wait right here." And she did, in the confidence that her father had never broken his promise before.

REFLECT

My daughter and I returned home that evening. My wife and I helped her get settled and ready for bed. As we tucked her into bed, her mother and I sat on either side and looked at our beautiful little girl who only moments before had been in such a serious accident. We came close that day to losing her. All of us took a moment to breath in that safety of sitting there on the edge of our daughter's bed. We kissed her on the forehead, read her a story from her favorite book (*The Chronicles of Narnia*), and watched her fall asleep.

As I closed the door of my daughter's bedroom, I couldn't help but think of the little girl in the next cubicle earlier that afternoon. I wondered whether anyone had taken the time to walk her to the door, if anyone made sure she that was comfortable on the ride home, if anyone had tucked her into bed or read her favorite story. And I wondered whether anyone had kissed her forehead and told her that it would all be OK.

I couldn't help but think how fragile the human condition really is. Yet as fragile as we may be, it is also fairly simple. We are built to need one another. We crave community. We come into this world needing someone to cover us, love us, stroke us, and tell us the dark shadows are just that, and then reassure us that morning will come soon. We need people to live up to their responsibilities and be faithful. We need for others to expect no less from us.

In John 14, Jesus takes a break from the mission field and speaks to the hearts of his followers. The message is simple and rather personal. "In my Father's house are many rooms ... and I go and prepare a place for you." The God of the universe, with all that was unfolding and with all that his own Son was facing, made the case that we belonged to God, and, even more importantly, that Jesus had taken the responsibility of our safety and care upon himself.

We learn about our responsibility for each other in watching God's care for us. There is no mistake in God's direct connection to not only our spiritual future, but to our lives, concerns, and dreams. God invested himself directly into our journey and even gave the life of his Son to insure its safe passage.

God teaches us responsibility for one another in several ways. First, God teaches us the importance of belonging and place. I never fully appreciated the importance of home until I had to leave one I had built. No, I am not talking about my "family" but an actual house my wife and I built several years ago. We lived in this particular community for fourteen years and grew to love the people very much. I liked to say that their DNA fit ours in so many ways. However, one part I took for granted was the actual place I called home.

Jesus talked a lot about place during his ministry. He visited his home often, was in the homes of friends and loved ones, and spoke of the special place Jerusalem had for all of them. Place mattered to Jesus. One of the responsibilities Jesus taught us was to value place.

And place spoke to more than just a house or a building or a street. It spoke to the "center of our universe." All of us have one. It doesn't have to be an actual place, but everyone has somewhere that speaks to our souls more clearly than anyone or any other place can. That is why Jesus talked about a "mansion," a home, and place.

Second, God teaches us responsibility for each other by preparing us to connect to appropriate places, people, and purposes. I loved going to my grandmother's house when I was younger. She would treat me like a king, always cooking whatever I wanted and making sure that I had anything I needed. But she spent an incredible amount of time getting ready for my arrival. I always had something "new." Yes, she spoiled me. But when people would mention this to her, she would always answer the same way. "Well, he is mine to spoil!" I never fully appreciated that answer until I was older and my grandmother was no longer with me. I didn't appreciate that she saw it as her responsibility to spoil her grandson.

Jesus said, "I go and prepare a place for you. . . ." It is God's joy to make a place for us, to spoil us.

Third, God teaches responsibility for each other by reminding us to welcome one another. Several years ago, I walked into a small church in the foothills of the Smokey Mountains in North Carolina. It was the perfect picture of a white-frame church, where the trees and flowers blossomed and, despite a brisk morning, the sun flew over the mountains as though announcing the day with a shout.

I was not preaching at the church. My family and I were on vacation and decided to attend a church that Sunday morning. We had picked out a church to attend, but in an age before every vehicle had a GPS, we couldn't locate it. We "happened" upon this little church as our "second choice."

From the moment we stepped into the small sanctuary, members intent on making us feel welcome surrounded us. Sure, it might have been the realization that a church that small, that far off the beaten path did not get many visitors. But the "feel" was something else. These folks welcomed us like family.

I have heard the term *family chapel* thrown around in an attempt to describe the small membership churches "culture." It is not always used as a flattering description. But there are worse things than being called "family." Of course, that was tongue-in-cheek. The "family chapel" is nice, especially when people actually treat you . . . like family. Can you think of something better than being welcomed home by someone who loves you? "And I will receive you unto myself . . . that where I am you will be also" (see John 14:3).

Fourth, God teaches us responsibility for each other by expecting us to be honest with one another. No one, and I can't say this loudly or boldly enough, tells you the truth like family. I have a great extended family whom I don't see nearly enough. I love them very much, but the schedule of daily routines shifts the focus of gatherings and opportunities to be together. When we are together, the story plays out in similar ways. We begin with the niceties of life—how the kids are doing, how the jobs are going, what seems to be coming next. We then move to old stories, usually the same ones, about things I did as a child or ways I embarrassed the family. It is brutal, particularly if there are those who hear these stories whom you would prefer not to hear them. A first cousin you played war with, or set the barn on fire with, gets special range for where his or her stories can go.

But after some time, the conversation becomes more complicated. We begin to talk about family relationships that are not going so well or that we have left long in need. We talk about where we could do better, where we let each other down, and where we could make it up to each other if there was an opportunity. Yes, we usually have difficult tones, straightforward words, and interesting banter, but the result is always the same. We end up hugging, telling each other "I love you," and moving on. There is nothing like family . . . telling you the truth. I don't always want to hear it, but we all need people who will tell us the tie is ugly, our breath stinks, the speck of food on our lip didn't go away with the napkin wipe, and our mistakes still need to be made well. We also need folks who will love us no matter what any of the above finally looks like.

Jesus said, "If it were not so, would I have told you that I go to prepare a place for you?" This passage may be the most underused and underappreciated verse in Scripture. Here is the Son of God, the Creator of the universe, saying to little ol' you and me that he would always shoot straight with us. We would never have to wonder where we are in God's presence, and we should never forget that, at the end of the day, we are family. Jesus taught us responsibility for each other by teaching us to be honest.

Many Americans list loneliness as one of their top-ten fears—not war, poverty, economic collapse, or nuclear annihilation. It is the morning, the day, the evening when they might not have anyone to share it with. With all we deal with, with all the issues that dominate the landscape, what causes a person to pick loneliness as such a great fear in his or her life? The answer is simple. We fear most what we miss most when life turns upside down.

We are responsible for one another. We are God's children. We are family.

REFINE

Read Genesis 1:1-3; 3:12-13; Matthew 5:13-16; John 14; and Acts 2:42-47; 5:7.

1. **Examine:** After reading the suggested Scriptures, examine what God is saying through these passages concerning your situation. What does God say about the importance of living faithful to our responsibilities? How do the passages of Scripture provide a new path and potential for how we confront living faithful to the responsibilities for our lives?

2. **Identify:** Identify the power of your responsibilities for your brother and sister in Christ, your neighbor. How has it affected your relationships? How do your current responsibilities affect the way you see God and serve God? How do these responsibilities affect the way you view the future and opportunities? Provide as detailed an explanation for the issue that holds you back.

3. **Define:** Define what a solution would look like if God truly dealt in the midst of your responsibilities for others. Many times, our inability to take hold of God's gift of healing, new direction, or second chance is our struggle in naming what those characteristics look like in our lives. We become so focused on the problem that we forget what a solution might entail. What will your relationships look like? What new opportunities will come your way? How will you serve God better? Define your solution. Be as specific as possible. Paint an unmistakable picture of how God reframes your responsibilities for others into a beautiful new masterpiece.

4. **Name:** Name the steps to achieve that solution. What would that desired future for God's new reality in your life require of you? What changes do you need to make to begin the process? What old patterns need addressing? What new habits should you take up? Name the process that becomes God's path to reshape your potential and your life.

5. **Commit:** Commit to an action plan to make God's plan your reality. When do you start? Who goes with you? How do you begin? Now start!

RESPOND

The following daily reading schedule provides insight for addressing the importance of living faithful to the responsibilities of your life. The goal is to watch God take the obstacles that keep you from your path in God and reshape your potential and possibilities.

Study Suggestions
1. Read each day's Scripture passage.
2. List the principle lessons of that day's Scripture.
3. Describe how the principles can be applied to your daily life.
4. Journal your thoughts, feelings, and impressions. Include a list of prayer requests, praises, and concerns.

Monday: Matthew 27:15-26
Tuesday: Numbers 1:50-51

Wednesday: Galatians 6:7-8
Thursday: Romans 12:6-8
Friday: 1 John 4:7-17
Saturday: Matthew 25:29

Prayer

Gracious God, we pray for those places where we have not lived up to our responsibilities, where we have let down those we love most, or where we have failed to be obedient to you. Give us courage to hold the banner of grace and forgiveness high. Give us joy to proclaim a new day of your good news. Give us compassion to meet the needs of those who hunger in body and soul. Gracious God, give us yourself that we might never forget what we are called do as a result of whose we are. You are our beautiful task, our objective, our ambition, and our reason for living. We love that you see us so differently than we oftentimes see ourselves. Thank you for taking this broken, jagged piece of our souls and for creating a beautiful masterpiece; in Christ. Amen.

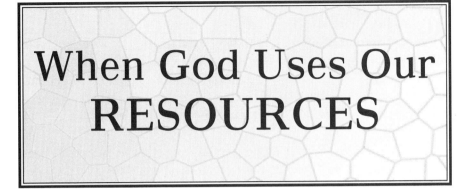

When God Uses Our RESOURCES

Scripture: Read Proverbs 3:9-10 and Malachi 3:6-12.

REVEAL

All of us have those gifts we buy at Christmas that are for the individuals for whom we feel responsible to buy a gift, but under normal circumstances probably would not. You know what I am talking about—the employer, committee member, teacher, and so forth who gets a gift out of obligation, although you know that you probably won't put much time into choosing it and that he or she most probably will never use it. This is the "dirty Santa" gift at the office party, or the "name out of the hat" at the Sunday school gathering. Regardless, we don't put much time into it, and, when we are on the receiving end, we really don't know what to do with it. In fact, I would bet that most "re-gifting" happens as a result of these type of gifts.

One Christmas, we had purchased our tenth such gift of the season when my wife asked, "Why do we do this?" The answer seemed obvious. "Because its Christmas, and people expect a gift." That was my reply anyway, although as I said it, it sounded as shallow as you just read.

"Really?" was my wife's comment. "We buy a gift that we really don't want to buy, that we don't put much effort into selecting, and give it to a person we would not normally give a gift to…because of an obligation?"

51

After a few moments of silence, and wondering whether there was a trick involved in her question, I replied, "Yes."

"Well, that is the dumbest thing I have ever heard," my wife shot back.

I wasn't sure how I had become responsible for meaningless Christmas gifts around the world and the act of re-gifting, in general; but I had. Actually, I had wondered the same thing many times—trying to make sense of our need to impress people with the act of giving, although the meaning of it is sketchy at best.

We talked about other ideas for gifts, usually finding ourselves back to where we started. However, it was our oldest daughter who provided a great alternative. She had seen a report in the news about the number of children who die around the world of issues we could solve—hunger, poverty, and war. She said 14,000 children die every day because they do not get enough food or clean water. The statistic is staggering. In a world where Americans spend over $30 billion a year on diet products, we have children dying from hunger and dehydration.

One of our family mottos is "You can't do everything, so do something." Our daughter decided to put that motto to action. She came to us with an idea.

"I know what my something should be," she said. "I would like to help children have enough clean water to drink, and I think that I know how to solve the Christmas gift issue as well." We perked up.

Our daughter devised a plan whereby we would buy drink coasters. We would wrap a coaster in a ribbon and attach a note for the person receiving the gift to know that a donation had been made in his or her name to an organization that provided rehydration kits to dying children in under-resourced areas of the world. The note read, "Every time you place a cold drink on this coaster, know that a gift in your honor provided living water for a child in need."

Our daughter had even gone so far as to learn that the word for "water" in Swahili is *maji*. Therefore, our effort was named the Maji Project. That Christmas, our family gave dozens of coasters to friends and family. However, as people would receive the gift, they wanted to participate as well. So the next Christmas, our daughter organized the project, complete with a logo and specially printed coasters. For a gift of ten dollars, a person could help eleven children. What a gift—both directions!

Over the last five years, our daughter's Maji Project, with the help of Church World Service, has provided nearly 20,000 rehydration kits to children in need. It is not a huge amount, especially in relation to the massive work of other large organizations. But don't tell that to the 20,000 children who are alive today because of one little girl's desire to do something.

She didn't have much to offer—nothing, really. But she claimed the heart of a problem, and decided to find a solution. And if everyone would do his or her "something," anything is possible.

Our daughter's Maji Project reminded me that God uses our resources, however large or small, public or private, and transforms the world. God did it with a herder from Midian, a shepherd boy from Judah, a carpenter from Nazareth, and a group of fishermen from Galilee. And God can do it with us, too. God asks only that we provide what we have—freely—and God will take it from there.

REFLECT

The accounts of Jesus feeding the masses have become part of our children's Sunday school lore. Most of us remember the story of the little boy who brings Jesus the fishes and loaves. In one account, Jesus feeds five thousand (Matthew 16; Mark 6; Luke 9; and John 6). In another, he feeds an additional four thousand (Matthew 15 and Mark 8). The numbers, particularly for Jesus' day, are staggering. Feeding thousands of people is a major event even today, using our food services technology. Put the whole scenario on a Galilean hillside two thousand years ago, and it becomes incredible.

But actually, two miracles happen in these passages. The first is that Jesus takes the meager offering of fishes and loaves and does something profound with them. The act of the miracle itself is worth the lesson. But for the second miracle, Jesus teaches the disciples and his followers lessons about the power of offering our resources to God. True to form, we walk along with valuable lessons to use in our lives.

The first lesson Jesus taught his followers was to notice the needs of others around them. In both accounts of Jesus feeding the masses, he recognized the people first. He saw their spiritual hunger, but he chose to respond to their physical hunger first. Jesus realized the people were weary and in need. Before he spoke to their souls, he dealt with their stomachs.

Many times, we hold our resources tightly living only in a spirit of self-interest. We can't see past our own wants to notice the needs of our brothers and sisters.

The second lesson Jesus taught his followers was to use the resources they had, not to whine about what they didn't have. In both accounts of Jesus feeding the masses, he instructs the disciples to bring him what they had. When they did, their offering was meager and insufficient, according to the world. Jesus broke the elements of fishes and loaves, much like he would break the bread in the upper room, and gave the elements for distribution. God makes what we possess, no matter how large or small, sacred and usable.

If the focus is on what we do not have instead of whatever gifts God has blessed us with, we add the spirit of insufficiency to our spirit of self-interest, making the issue even more about us. Jesus makes our gifts holy by his presence, by his touch, by his example in treasuring their earthly value.

The third lesson Jesus taught his followers was to make the sharing of our resources an act of community, not just an act of charity. The accounts of Jesus feeding the masses reads more like a covered-dish luncheon or fellowship dinner than a soup kitchen. In fact, the lesson here is that any time God uses our resources, the goal will always be to bring God's children closer, and not only to meet the needs of others, but to continue breaking down the barriers that separate us in the first place. In doing so, Jesus teaches how community reduces our propensity for separating ourselves on the basis of possessions.

For many in the church, it becomes easy to write a check as a means of relinquishing our duty to our brothers and sisters. Jesus taught us that we belong to the same family, and that makes every person welcome at every table. We would no more give our child a check when he or she needs a hug. We would no more only give our child a hug when he or she needs a meal.

The final lesson Jesus taught his followers was that *all* our resources matter, and that none should be wasted. This lesson from the accounts of Jesus feeding the masses reminds us that gifts, either by our own or others' assessments, always matter and are significant in allowing the good news to unfold in real ways for real people in real places. The Scriptural passages state that "people ate to their fill" and that baskets of food were left over. When God uses our resources, needs are met. And those blessings pass along from one person to the next because such grace cannot be contained.

Today it is easy to make an act of good will or good works a snapshot of time and effect. But in reality, when God uses our lives to meet the needs of others, those blessings overflow and spill into places we could never imagine.

Speaking of Gifts

Every Christian has a spiritual gift that, when used, shares the good news in a unique way, designed especially by the Holy Spirit for that person. When we don't employ our spiritual gifts, God finds others to fill that need. However, no one will meet that need the way God intended for us to meet that need.

From every angle of our spiritual journey, God uses our resources of gifts, materials, abilities, spirit, and dreams to frame and shape the gospel in our world. We are not bit players in a drama that has no meaning. We are children of the Creator, divinely endowed and engaged to meet the needs of those around us with the gifts we have been given so that all should "be filled" to abundance.

Abundance is a powerful and important term for those of us who believe and follow Christ. We often live lives of scarcity, not just in our material world, but also for the ways God has ordained us to participate in others coming to know Christ. When we live from a point of scarcity, we retreat into the shadows of our own needs, missing the needs of those around us. When we live from a point of scarcity, no one, including ourselves, ever has "what we need."

Abundance turns the tables on scarcity. Sure, we deal with the needs of a world so often divided by what we do not have instead of approaching such issues, our lives, and our relationships by the light of what we all have in Christ. Jesus said, "I have come that you may have life, and have it more abundantly" (see John 10:10). And you can take that promise "to the bank."

REFINE

Read Job 36:30-32; Matthew 15; Mark 8; Luke 9; 12:14-16; John 6; and 2 Peter 1:1-3.

1. **Examine:** After reading the suggested Scriptures, examine what God is saying through these passages concerning your situation.

What does God say about the potential of resources? How do the passages of Scripture provide a new path and potential for how we use our resources?

2. **Identify:** Identify the issues of properly using resources. How have these issues affected your relationships? How do the use and priority of resources affect the way you see God and serve him? How does the use of your resources affect the way you view the future and opportunities? Provide a detailed explanation for an issue that holds you back.

3. **Define:** Define what a solution would look like if God worked in the midst of utilizing your resources. Many times, our inability to take hold of God's gift of healing, new direction, or second chance is our struggle in naming what those characteristics look like in our lives. We become so focused on the problem that we forget what a solution might entail. What will your relationships look like? What new opportunities will come your way? How will you serve God better? Define your solution! Be as specific as possible. Paint an unmistakable picture of how God reframes your use of resources into a beautiful new masterpiece.

4. **Name:** Name the steps to achieve that solution. What would that desired future for God's new reality in your life require of you? What changes do you need to make to begin the process? What old patterns need addressing? What new habits should you take up? Name the process that becomes God's path to reshape your potential and your life.

5. **Commit:** Commit to an action plan to make God's plan your reality. When do you start? Who goes with you? How do you begin? Now start!

RESPOND

The following daily reading schedule provides insight for addressing the proper use of resources in your life. The goal is to watch God take the unrealized potential that keeps you from your path in God and reshape your potential and possibilities.

Study Suggestions

1. Read each day's Scripture passage.
2. List the principle lessons of that day's Scripture.
3. Describe how the principles can be applied to your daily life.
4. Journal your thoughts, feelings, and impressions. Include a list of prayer requests, praises, and concerns.

Monday: John 3:16-17
Tuesday: Luke 21:1-4
Wednesday: Psalm 54:6
Thursday: 2 Corinthians 9:10-11
Friday: 1 Peter 4:10
Saturday: Proverbs 3:9-10

Prayer

Gracious God, we pray for the places where we have withheld the gifts you have given us or used them for the wrong reasons. You have shared your heart, gifting each of us with ways that not only bring us closer to you, but to one another as well. Yet we set them down, give them away, or sell them to the lowest bidder. Your gifts transform our lives. Our gifts transform the world. You are our treasure. We love that you see us so differently than we oftentimes see ourselves. Thank you for taking this broken, jagged piece of our souls and for creating a beautiful masterpiece; in Christ. Amen.

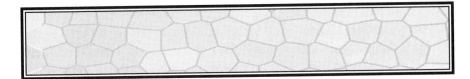

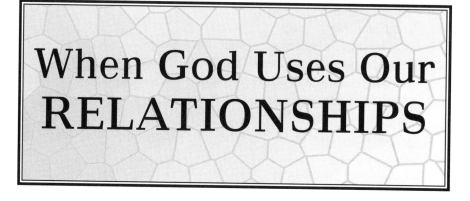

When God Uses Our RELATIONSHIPS

Scripture: Read Matthew 27:57-61 and Mark 5.

REVEAL

Recently, I was a guest on a nationally syndicated radio program whose core message is about cultivating healthy families. This particular ministry is one of the leading organizations in developing resources for spiritually growing those relationships most important to us.

Two to four episodes of the program are recorded each week, usually with two guests an episode. As with other media appearances, the guests meet with the hosts beforehand to go over the format of the program and the issues God has laid on our hearts to share within our own area of expertise.

As with other media appearances, I have had the chance to meet some fascinating individuals—Shaunti Feldhahn, Beth Moore, Sandi Patty, Josh Hamilton, and others. This week was no different. My fellow guest on the program was Donna Hughes. Donna is the founder and chair of a non-profit that ministers to those affected by addictions to pornography.

Her organization is doing an amazing work, reaching into the midst of a very dangerous, difficult topic for families today. I could not help but be impressed by her commitment and dedication to providing a biblical framework for how the church addresses issues of healthy, human sexuality.

But halfway through my conversation with Mrs. Hughes, I couldn't help but think that I had seen her before. She seemed very familiar to me, but I just could not place her. Just then, she made a profound statement—"the markers of life that often direct us do not have to be the markers that ultimately define us." In other words, although life can lead us (thus we lead ourselves and others) into unhealthy places, the Bible says that we do not have to stay there.

It was at that moment that I realized where I had seen Mrs. Hughes. Her maiden name was Rice, Donna Rice. Ms. Rice was a young woman caught at the center of one of the most public political scandals of the last 25 years.

Ms. Rice was in an inappropriate relationship with then-presidential candidate Senator Gary Hart. In 1987, she was young, naive, and, in her own words, broken from the outside edges to the center of her being. The scandal rocked the political world and ruined Senator Hart's career.

Ms. Rice became a household name—a symbol of bad decisions, impropriety, and the power of secrets that distract, derail, and destroy. She was humiliated and disgraced.

Over the next few years, Ms. Rice withdrew from the spotlight and reflected on her life. She had seen the most important relationships of her life change overnight and discovered how fragile friendships can be. Needless to say, many who had walked with Ms. Rice through other moments refused to be seen with her. But others stood by her in the midst of the fire. Ms. Rice learned whom she could truly count on.

Donna Rice (now Hughes) made some really complicated mistakes but learned from them. She turned her life around and married the love of her life. Mrs. Hughes started a ministry named "Enough Is Enough," which fights the rampant and dangerous effect of Internet pornography. She has appeared nationally and has become a voice for healthy families.

My meeting with Mrs. Hughes was delightful. She was transparent, honest, and very clear about how the difficulties of inappropriate and broken relationships shaped her life in negative ways. But she added, "Once I turned those relationships and patterns over to God, he took something so ugly and did something beautiful."

Relationships are powerful pieces, maybe the most powerful, of our life's frame of existence. We are created in relationship with a mother

59

and a father. We thrive in relationships through friendships that shape and guide us. We spend our lives looking for someone who completes that covenant fashioned in God's image. We mourn most deeply when those relationships that matter most break down or end.

So believing in a God who uses the pieces of our most incomplete and broken relationships not only recasts our interactions with others, but shapes the foundations for every other aspect of our lives. When our relationships break down, every other part of life becomes susceptible to the adversary's attacks. But the reverse is also true. We are strongest when we stand firm with those we love.

God wants to strengthen your relationships. God wants to put the broken ones together. Again, God wants to celebrate the joy of relationships working well. God uses the pieces from the best and worst of who we are "together" to create a masterpiece.

REFLECT

When we read the Gospels, it is easy for us to think of Jesus walking around the Palestinian countryside with his band of disciples merrily following behind. Jesus and the Twelve travel from one venue to another, stopping long enough on the mountainside, along the shore, or under a tree to dispense the word of wisdom for the day or to perform a miracle. OK, maybe not so easy!

First of all, the travel conditions were wearying and cumbersome; and Jesus' ministry territory stretched from one end of Jewish Palestine to another, occasionally even crossing into Gentile territories. As a traveling preacher, Jesus would have experienced a lot of discomfort. I'm sure he smelled, felt, and acted like any other weary traveler. Not exactly the clean and shiny image we have of the Messiah; but remember, he was fully human, too.

Second, like any traveler of his era, Jesus relied on the kindness of friends and supporters for the basic necessities. Scripture tells us that Jesus did not have a place to call his own (see Matthew 8:20; Luke 9:58), but instead counted on the hospitality of others to provide food, rest, and relaxation (see Mark 14:13-25; Luke 10:38). Given the geography that Jesus' ministry covered, it was convenient for him to have certain places he stayed whenever he was in a particular area. The home of Mary, Martha, and Lazarus in Bethany was one such place.

Third, because of his reliance on these stops and given the nomadic nature of Jesus' ministry back and forth across Palestine, he would have stopped frequently in these places. The relationships he developed with these particular followers would have been significant. Scripture tells us that Jesus felt at home with Mary, Martha, and Lazarus (see Luke 10:38-42; John 12:1-8). We can't be sure how and why they came to play such an important role in his ministry, but their support of and dedication to Jesus were unquestionable. Some accounts place Mary (possibly as a troubled young woman or even a person of ill repute) at the center of Jesus' connection to the family. Yet it's clear from the Gospels that Jesus loved not only Mary but also her sister and brother; and theirs was an enduring friendship. But this was more than a personal relationship. The family supported Jesus' ministry and vocation; and they hosted, on at least one occasion, others who came to hear Jesus teach (see Luke 10:38-42). Their home was more than a stopover for his travels; it was a teaching center as well. Jesus treated this family from Bethany as friends and considered them an important part of his ministry and life. It is clear that as much as they needed Jesus, Jesus also needed them and appreciated their care for him and his disciples.

Jesus built enduring relationships that went beyond the roles of teacher and student. We can't picture Jesus only as the rabbi marching through Galilee, spouting lessons for living. No, he built real relationships. Jesus had friends. Think about that for a moment. It is an important concept that many modern believers miss. If Jesus had friends, then he loved some folks more deeply than others. (Admit it; that idea makes you nervous!) I'm not referring to the grand, cosmic love that God has for each one of us—love that, by its very nature, cannot be more or less or play favorites. I'm talking about the love that any human has for another, especially if they have shared profound moments of success and struggle. It stands to reason that, if Jesus was fully human, as the Scriptures insist, and if he had people in his life who supported and cared for him during his ministry, then he would have had a deeper, personal connection to those folks. I tried out this theory on several minister friends of mine recently, and they reacted like jealous girlfriends. I was completely unprepared for how they resisted the notion that Jesus could have loved some friends more than others. When I asked them why the idea bothered them so much, they responded with theological arguments, including the impeccably logical (and my personal favorite), "Well, he's Jesus."

When I went so far as to point out that, in our ministries, we are all guilty of having parishioners to whom we feel closer than others, one friend, who may be the smartest of all of us, froze spiritually. (You could see it on his face!) He was able only to utter, "But we are human."

"Well, wasn't Jesus supposed to be human like us?" I questioned.

"Yes, but ...," he replied.

"But what?" I countered. "If Jesus was human, then ..."

"Yes, but ...," he replied again.

"But what?" I again countered. "If Jesus was human, then wouldn't he have loved some people more than others? What are you so worried about?"

My friend stood silent for a moment and then answered, "I'm just not sure that I like Jesus being that human."

The conversation got me thinking: If Jesus was human enough to need resources and a place to sleep during his earthly ministry, that means Jesus needed people to provide assistance. And if Jesus needed people, then the ones who responded to his needs would naturally see a more intimate side of him. And if they saw a more intimate side of a fully human Jesus, then would they not also experience the depth of his response for their care? And at such depths of personal relationship, would not Jesus call them friend? I mean *real* friends—not just a "friend of God" friend but also an "I've got your back" friend. As you know, there is a difference; and that difference affects us in profound ways. "I've got your back" friendships shape who we are and form the heart of what matters in our lives. I don't believe it was any different for Jesus. Jesus needed people. He needed friends. I believe that Mary, Martha, and Lazarus were these kinds of friends to Jesus; and I believe that he needed them and loved them very much.

The first lesson of this encounter is that Jesus needed people. Jesus had friends. Jesus teaches us that relationships are more than momentary connections; they mirror the very essence of who God created us to be. He not only talked about these connections, but he also lived them in his friendships with people like Mary, Martha, and Lazarus. And if such friendships are to mean anything in this world, they must also weather a hairline fracture or two in order to become invulnerable to change, disruption, and even death. (More about that in a minute.)

Why was it necessary for Jesus to walk among us in order to redeem us? Could it be that Jesus had to make friends and see imperfections and feel loss—just like we do—in order to accomplish his mission? Jesus always goes to the heart of what we dread in this world. We dread being alone, so we make friends. We dread being hurt, so we don't make friends. We dread feeling betrayed, so we don't let our real selves show. We dread loss, so we choose not to love. If Jesus' friendships teach us nothing else, they remind us that he understands the deepest, most personal needs we have. He became like us, not just to understand us, but to stand for us in the places we could not go.

REFINE

Read Matthew 27 and Mark 5.

1. **Examine:** After reading the suggested Scriptures, examine what God is saying through these passages concerning your current life situation. What does God say about the importance of living in healthy relationships? How do the passages of Scripture provide a new path and potential for how healthy relationships shape our lives?

2. **Identify:** Identify the power of healthy relationships—for you, your brother and sister in Christ, your neighbor. How do your current relationships affect the way you see God and serve him? How do these relationships affect the way you view the future and opportunities? Provide as detailed an explanation for the issue that holds you back.

3. **Define:** Define what a solution would look like if God were truly allowed to work in our relationships. Many times, our inability to take hold of God's gift of healing, new direction, or second chance is our struggle in naming what those characteristics look like in our lives. We become so focused on the problem that we forget what a solution might entail. What will your relationships look like if we allow God such access? What new opportunities will come your way? How will you serve God better? Define your solution! Be as specific as possible. Paint an unmistakable picture of how God reframes your relationships into a beautiful new masterpiece.

4. **Name:** Name the steps to achieve that solution. What would that desired future for God's new reality in your life require of you? What changes do you need to make to begin the process? What old patterns need addressing? What new habits should you take up? Name the process that becomes God's path to reshape your potential and your life.

5. **Commit:** Commit to an action plan to make God's plan your reality. When do you start? Who goes with you? How do you begin? Now start!

RESPOND

The following daily reading schedule provides insight for addressing the importance of living faithful to the relationships of your life. The goal is to watch God take the obstacles that keep you from your path in God and reshape your potential and possibilities.

Study Suggestions
1. Read each day's Scripture passage.
2. List the principle lessons of that day's Scripture.
3. Describe how the principles can be applied to your daily life.
4. Journal your thoughts, feelings, and impressions. Include a list of prayer requests, praises, and concerns.

Monday: 1 Samuel 18:1-4
Tuesday: Genesis 50:14-21
Wednesday: John 5:7
Thursday: Ephesians 4:32
Friday: Luke 22:7-20
Saturday: Matthew 27:32-61

Prayer
Gracious God, we pray for those places where our relationships have looked too much like the world and less like you. You created us in your image, to need each other so that our community might testify to the power of our covenant with you. Give us hope to hold the hands of those in need. Give us hearts to hear the cries of those who sit at the city gate.

Give us hallelujahs to sing your praises even when the world's melody can be heard. You are our Father, our Mother, our Friend. We love that you see us so differently than we oftentimes see ourselves. Thank you for taking this broken, jagged piece of our souls and for creating a beautiful masterpiece; in Christ. Amen.

After WORDS

The sky darkens, and a strange hue forms over the horizon. Although it is only noon, it seems as though life itself is being lost. The sight of it all drains their very breath. As the cross is lifted into place, Jesus' mother lets out a muffled cry. None can believe what they see—such a good man, such a good friend being tortured and, now, being killed. The mourners, the spectators, those drunk with the smell of death—it is almost more than any decent human being can endure.

Maybe that is why Jesus' first word shakes them so. "Father, forgive them; for they do not know what they are doing" (Luke 23:34). After everything, including the beating, the mockery of a trial, and now this, he asks for *their* forgiveness? At this point, forgiveness and justice seem two concepts very far apart.

For several hours there have been no other sounds—only the groans and desperate pleas of the two men hanging beside Jesus. Then everyone begins hurling insults at him—the guards, the leaders, even one of the criminals. But while the first criminal mocks him, shouting insults about saving the three of them, the other criminal finally says, "Do you not fear God, since you are under the same sentence of condemnation? And we indeed have been condemned justly, for we are getting what we deserve for our deeds, but this man has done nothing wrong." Then the criminal turns to Jesus. "Remember me when you come into your kingdom" Jesus turns his head toward his defender and says, "Truly I tell you, today you will be with me in Paradise" (Luke 23:40-43).

Everyone knows that Jesus is close to his mother. Their relationship of love and great care is evident. They have experienced the traditional mother-son conversations; and at times, Jesus proceeds down paths of which Mary does not approve. But especially in these final moments, no one doubts his or her love for each other. That is why when Jesus lifts his head to speak to her, for any parent or child, the scene becomes almost unbearable. He nods toward John and says, "Woman, here is your son." Then, looking at John, he adds, "Here is your mother" (John 19:26b-27a). It is remarkable that, given all that is taking place, Jesus stops to make sure that his mother is cared for. For many, it seems odd that Jesus would be worried about such matters; but for those who know him, it makes all the sense in the world.

As the hours move on, Jesus raises his head, but instead of addressing someone around the cross, his voice trails upward. The scream is startling: "My God, my God, why have you forsaken me?" (Matthew 27:46). For a man of such faith, the words seem out of place. Some think that he is calling Elijah; but for those who have journeyed with him and now stand at a distance, the words seem almost palpable, and they are clearly addressed to God. What sadness his disciples must have felt— first, for their dying teacher and friend, but also because they have never witnessed anyone so alone.

Then, almost as a concession, Jesus looks to the guards standing at the foot of the cross and says, "I am thirsty" (John 19:28). Although many fail to understand what this means, Jesus knows; and as the syllables roll from his mouth, the words of the psalmist are fulfilled: "My strength has dried up like sunbaked clay. / My tongue sticks to the roof of my mouth. / You have laid me in the dust and left me for dead" (Psalm 22:15, NLT). After everything, Jesus has nothing left to give.

Finally Jesus raises his head one last time and says, "It is finished" (John 19:30). "Into your hands I commend my spirit" (Luke 23:46). For what seems an eternity, the world shakes. Rocks fall, all the guards but one vanish, and the sightseers run for cover. When the excitement subsides, only the women remain, standing firmly but distant from the cross. Rumors abound about these last, unbelievable moments. Some say the veil in the Temple tears at the exact moment Jesus dies; others claim that the dead are raised. Regardless, something remarkable has happened. Crucifixion is supposed to take longer, most times ending with the breaking of the criminal's legs. But that does not happen with Jesus. In one final miracle, he simply allows himself to die. In the chaos that follows, most do not even realize what they have seen, except for one Roman soldier, who looks to the cross and utters, "Truly this man was God's Son!" (Matthew 27:54). Ironically, after three years of ministry, preaching, miracles, and change, at the end, it is one Gentile who truly understands.

Soon, it will be time to take him down. The burial will require assistance, but after all the confusion and fear of the past twenty-four hours, who would dare help? Mary, Jesus' mother, thinks, *He came into the world without a place to lay his head; now, in his death, we have no place to lay his body.* But someone has seen Joseph of Arimathea, and he promises to assist them—a Pharisee, no less. He recoils in horror at the past hours, ashamed and distraught at all that has happened.

For the disciples, their next steps are uncertain. Their world shattered, their hearts aching, they wonder, *Why go on at all?* But their faith gives them an inner strength, and they know life must continue. Besides, Jesus would have expected no less. Whatever it takes, they must make sure they care for Jesus, for that is exactly what he had done for them. They certainly will not abandon him. Still, the echo of his last words ring within them: "It is finished."

How could they know that actually it has just begun?

(Adapted from *The Seven Next Words of Christ,* by Shane Stanford [Abingdon Press, 2006]; used and adapted by permission.)

———————

I wrote these words several years ago as part of my book *The Seven Next Words of Christ.* Over the years, I have read them many times at the end of the season of Lent as a reminder of the picture that unfolded that dark, lonely Friday afternoon at a place called Golgotha.

For most of my life, I saw these events as part of a wider celebration of joy attached to an Easter morning filled with light, love, and new "Sunday, church-going clothes." It was easy to overlook the hours of the previous days because the empty tomb made everything better and seemed right.

But several years ago, while standing in an empty, dark church after a Good Friday service, it occurred to me that we rush through these last days of the Lenten season too quickly, mostly as a race to Easter, but maybe for something else sitting at the bottom of our souls. I don't like death. I don't like the dark. I don't like loneliness. All of these attributes landed on that "hill far away" some two thousand years ago; and worse yet, as I pondered those moments, standing in the dark of that lonely sanctuary, it hit me that all of this happened to someone I professed to love. It occurred to me that if this had been my spouse, my daughter, or my best friend, I would stand at that place for years to come, mourning that this intersection of time changed my life forever.

Of course, two things are very different about this situation with this Jesus, my friend. First, I know how the story ends. I know that two mornings later, another friend from Scripture finds the tomb empty. I like focusing on that part of the story more. But second, Resurrection is easier; it is neat. I don't have to rummage around in the basement of my spirit arranging the good and bad, broken and whole, wondering whether what I have found (and what he might find) really matters. So I skipped over the last part of Lent, eager to find Sunday morning.

However, standing in that darkened sanctuary, I realized the importance of Friday, the reason the tomb is made powerful because of the bitter loss of the cross. I realized that in rushing over the Crucifixion, I was denying myself something more for the Resurrection. The empty grave means something to all of us (or it should). It means something more when viewed through the lens of Calvary.

Remember the first story of this journey together. We left Dwight Eisenhower making the decision to send young men across the channel in one of the most important battles of human history. But there is more to the story. Generals George Marshall and Dwight Eisenhower shaped the arc of the twentieth century. As much as any other men, these icons of the US military defined the outcome of not only a war but a generation of freedom versus tyranny. Today, they are legends, revered with highest esteem.

A wonderful picture taken toward the end of their careers shows the two giants sitting together, talking over days gone by. By this time, it seemed they "walked above the clouds," as one historian friend likes to say. And today, we press our faces against the window frames of history and marvel at what these two men accomplished—winning a world war, restructuring Europe, assuming the presidency. We land at these markers of their lives because we like to cheer our heroes and say, "Well done!"

However, to understand George Marshall or Dwight Eisenhower, one has to look past the military accolades and gigantic accomplishments. No, to understand either of these men and what drove them to become the men we celebrate and revere, it is important to look at the underbelly of their journeys—journeys that led both of them through the best and worst that life has to offer.

For instance, George Marshall lost his first wife to a heart condition at a young age. Her death was sudden and shocking. In confiding to a friend, General Marshall said that he could not envision a future or how to make decisions for tomorrow in light of these circumstances. He felt paralyzed and unable to go forward. He survived by throwing himself into his work.

Dwight Eisenhower, whose life has been reviewed from every angle, considered the death of his young son Doud to be one of (if not the most) important events of his life. Doud died of scarlet fever in a time when treatment was limited. His son's death profoundly affected Eisenhower, changing his marriage and pushing his daily schedule to a pattern that would break most men. (*Partners in Command: George Marshall and Dwight Eisenhower in War and Peace*, by Mark Perry [Penguin Books, 2007]; pp. 41, 44, 46, 71, 296, 307, and 412.)

Two men, completely dedicated to their responsibilities at a time when the world hung in the balance; but also two men, propelled to these legendary places through incredibly dark passages. You can't understand the accolades of George Marshall or Dwight Eisenhower without looking around the corner at their most broken times and places.

Sunday matters. It changed us. It changed history. But the glory and power of Sunday happens against the backdrop of the loss and pain of Friday noon. The majesty of the Resurrection is that God worked a masterpiece that early morning, filled with beautiful images of forgiveness, life, hope, and the calling of our names by one who really knows us. Yet the Resurrection's masterpiece emerges on the canvas of death, hopelessness, abandonment, and the forgotten places that usually make us wince. But that is why we glare at them now. That is why we stand with these shards of life scattered around us watching God, piece by piece, take the events of Friday and craft them together into a mosaic of the best of eternity.

We should not want to understand legendary leaders without knowing the dark nights of their souls that make them who they are. We should not want to see the masterpiece unless we understand how the colors and images unfold in an explosion of depth and dimension. And we should not want to journey to Easter without pausing just long enough at Calvary to peer at one form of jagged rock before we roll the stones away.

My friend, God makes the masterpiece of you and me come together. The pieces fit again. God takes our journey of life and makes it mean something, gently forming the mosaic of our broken places into something beautiful.